The Associated Press Guide to

PUNCTUATION

ALSO BY
THE ASSOCIATED PRESS

*The Associated Press
Guide to Internet Research
and Reporting*

*The Associated Press
Stylebook and Briefing
on Media Law*

AP Associated Press

The Associated Press Guide to

PUNCTUATION

Rene J. Cappon

BASIC
BOOKS

A Member of the Perseus Books Group
New York

Many of the designations used by manufacturers and sellers to distinguish their products are claimed as trademarks. Where those designations appear in this book and Basic Books was aware of a trademark claim, the designations have been printed in initial capital letters.

Copyright © 2003 by The Associated Press
Previously published by Perseus Publishing
Published by Basic Books,
A Member of the Perseus Books Group
http://www.basicbooks.com

All rights reserved. No part of this publication may be reproduced, stored in a retrieval system, or transmitted, in any form or by any means, electronic, mechanical, photocopying, recording, or otherwise, without the prior written permission of the publisher. Printed in the United States of America.

Library of Congress Control Number: 2002112483
ISBN 0–7382–0785–3

Books published by Basic Books are available at special discounts for bulk purchases in the U.S. by corporations, institutions, and other organizations. For more information, please contact the Special Markets Department at the Perseus Books Group, 11 Cambridge Center, Cambridge, MA 02142, or call (800) 255–1514 or (617)252–5298, or e-mail j.mccrary@perseusbooks.com.

Text design by Lisa Kreinbrink
Set in 10-point Bookman by
the Perseus Books Group

First printing, January 2003
MV   05 06   10 9 8

CONTENTS

The Associated Press Guide to

PUNCTUATION

Chapter 1
INTRODUCTION

Punctuation in skilled hands is a remarkably subtle system of signals, signs, symbols and winks that keep readers on the smoothest road.

Too subtle, perhaps: Has any critic or reviewer ever praised an author for being a master of punctuation, a virtuoso of commas? Has anyone ever won a Pulitzer, much less a Nobel, for elegant distinctions between dash and colon, semicolon and comma?

In the word business, punctuation is considered a given (it isn't, and actually takes thought). So perhaps it's true, as has been long rumored, that some respected authors leave punctuation to such inferior beings as editors and proofreaders.

What does punctuation actually do? That's what this little book is about, but, in general, punctuation links or separates sentences and their elements, avoids ambiguities, clarifies meanings and sometimes refines them.

As a small example, the lowly hyphen differentiates a *small business association* (a small group) from a *small-business association* (a group composed of small businesses). The hyphen shows what words need to be read as one.

More complicated, commas spell the difference between essential clauses (vital to the meaning) from nonessential clauses, adding peripheral description or information.

Necessary as it is (try writing a passage without punctuation), word people hardly ever fly into a passion on the subject, as they would over points of grammar and word choice.

That's not because punctuation resembles the peaceable kingdom where everything is settled. As Theodore Bernstein has said in "The Careful Writer":

"About the only thing writers and editors agree on . . . is that a period is placed at the end of a declarative sentence . . . and that a question mark is placed at the end of a sentence that genuinely asks a question."

Oddly, the disagreements have produced little turbulence. One of the few disputes that resembled a controversy involved the question of whether a comma should go before the "and" in the final term of a series: "Tom, Dick, and Harry." The great majority decided to forgo the comma. A minority kept it, and both went their own way.

The fact is that publications, usually ensconced behind their own stylebooks, do their own thing without polemics or efforts at conversion. Styles simply differ (and readers, I suspect, are none the wiser).

Some authorial eccentricities, however, could hardly escape attention. Gertrude Stein generally avoided punctuation lest it distract from her words. (Most readers would have found her words distracting enough.)

James Joyce had no use for quotation marks—he used dashes instead—and the entire long soliloquy of Molly Bloom at the end of "Ulysses" is innocent of punctuation, compounding confusion among readers' minds.

George Bernard Shaw, a writer of great force and clarity, took a dislike to the apostrophe.

He spelled contractions "dont," "couldnt," "wont," "doesnt," as it appears in all his printed works. And the poet E.E. Cummings found capital letters offensive and printed everything in lowercase.

━ ━

For many millenniums, language meant speech and speech only. Not until some Mesopotamian spoilsports devised a workable alphabet did writing make the scene, albeit in cuneiform and solely for commercial use or to lavish fulsome praise on kings and kinglets.

It took several more millenniums before writing spread from a handful of clerics and learned elites into a common blessing of selected cultures.

But written words, however sophisticated, never threatened the supremacy of speech as the arbiter of language change. That still holds true.

Take the adverb "hopefully," if you can bear it. Language critics and commentators condemned it vociferously, but it became common in speech—and is now common in writing, too.

It's similar to many vainly proscribed words. "Snuck," for "sneak," is among the latest.

Besides its impregnable position as the conductor of language usage, speech held another advantage over writing, and that was clarity. Hearers could seldom misunderstand the speaker, for speech has a prodigious non-verbal arsenal: pitch, pause, stress, intonation, facial expression, gesture, body language.

It was to make up for the loss of speech accouterments that punctuation gradually developed. The idea goes back hundreds of years, furthered powerfully by the invention of movable type and the early printers of the 15th century. The Gutenberg Bible already had periods, commas and colons.

Like most style matters, punctuation changed over the years. In earlier days, it reflected spoken delivery, carefully marking places where speakers and readers had to take a breath. The so-called breath comma, an annoyance to the fastidious, survived well into the era when nobody read aloud anymore.

Punctuation today is oriented to the grammatical rather than the rhetorical, and it conforms to the modern principle that less is more. We punctuate conservatively, avoid all surplus.

By our standards, the literary lights of the 17th and 18th centuries indulged in lavish overpunctuation.

Commas, colons, semicolons, even dashes pop up wildly in spots where we would never place them. Commas habitually appear before "that" clauses that we leave alone. Two examples from Samuel Johnson: "It is not improbably, that Shakespeare put . . ." and "The only passage, by which it could be entered, was a cavern . . . "

Somebody took the trouble to count overwrought punctuation in a letter by Lord Chesterfield, valued for his style. In 50 sentences, he counted 45 semicolons, 8 colons, and no fewer than 193 commas.

That's overdone by our lights, to put it mildly. But we should remember also that the age of overpunctuation was also the age of Swift, Pope, Dryden, Addison, Steele, Boswell, Jonson and other literary giants.

Rene J. Cappon
The Associated Press

Chapter 2
THE AMPERSAND

Not many people know the word, but everybody knows the sign *(&)* that stands for "and."

The ampersand apparently was invented in the 17th century, and was once widely used as a space-saver.

Nowadays, it should be confined to names that formally contain it: *AT&T, Newport News Shipping & Dry Dock Co.*

The ampersand ranks first among punctuation marks by virtue of the alphabet, but its significance is last.

Chapter 3

THE APOSTROPHE

The apostrophe is an alphabetical neighbor to the ampersand, but is far more versatile. Anything but a slug would be.

People may laugh at the grimly limited ampersand, but nobody laughs at the apostrophe. One of its main jobs is to ride herd on possessives, which is serious business, indeed.

So serious, in fact, that the Oxford Companion to English Literature observes glumly: "There never was a golden age in which the rules for the possessive apostrophe were clearcut and known, understood, and followed by most educated people."

I cannot hope to reconstruct a golden age that never existed, but I can offer some basic guidelines to contemporary usage. Granted, they aren't universally accepted—few elements of punctuation are—but I'll happily sidestep grammarian disputes.

Besides forming possessives, the apostrophe also forms some plurals, indicates the omission of letters and numbers, and treats gerunds with grammatical civility.

That's quite a bulging backpack, as you'll find. But first, I want to deal with a resounding negative.

ON GUARD! Let's dispatch this spook right away: a misuse of the apostrophe that makes for one of the most gruesome errors in written English. To wit:

"Its" is a possessive. "It's" is a contraction (for "it is"). You'd think it's impossible to confuse, but to the embarrassment of all concerned, it happens: *Its (it's) an important event; Russia and it's (its) largest oil company.* . . .

And, to avoid similar disasters, never, never inject an apostrophe into other pronouns, such as mine, yours, your, ours, his, hers, theirs, whose.

Anyone who wants to sound REALLY illiterate need only emulate those clueless Brits who

drove retired copy editor John Richard to co-
found The Apostrophe Protection Society.

It was more than he could bear to keep
reading "Apple's and pear's for sale" on grocery
signs, and "Chip's and Pea's" offered on menu
boards in many pubs.

Richard's society sends polite letters to of-
fenders setting them straight on the difference
between plural and possessive. The United
States is not immune: "Menu's change
weekly," we read, and "specially selected
item's." Maybe we need a branch of Richard's
group here.

Plain Possessives. By "plain," I mean words
that do NOT end in *s: Jack's hovel, Jill's palace,
Joe's costly sneakers, Bush's ranch, the gover-
nor's obtuseness, Einstein's theories, the president's perks, Frankenstein's monster* (yes, the
monster wasn't Frankenstein but Frankenstein's creation). These forms are in constant
use and cause little trouble.

***S*-Endings.** Usually plurals. *Girls' wardrobes,
bureaucrats' bewilderment, senators' quarrels,*

janitors' strike, workers' rights. You simply add the '.

Names Ending in *S*.   Singulars, that is. Again, just add the apostrophe: *Achilles' heel, Socrates' question, Jesus' parables, Hercules' labors, Oedipus' blindness, Dickens' characters, Kansas' flatlands, Moses' wanderings, Tennessee Williams' plays, Xerxes' armies, Yeats' poems, Keats' odes.*

Irregular Plurals   also take the apostrophe: *children's hour, women's rights, gentlemen's traditions, men's club,* and so do nouns that are the same in singular or plural: *the single moose's antlers, the deer's track, the two corps' travels.* The apostrophe stays whether the meaning is singular or plural.

Special Words   that are in plural form but mean the singular: *politics' pitfalls, mathematics' difficulties, measles' dangers, physics' problems.* The punctuation is solid, but these constructions don't read well. You do better with "the pitfalls OF politics," "the difficulties OF mathematics."

Gerund Possessives.   A gerund is an *-ing* word that looks like a participle but acts as a noun. "His mother knew he was swimming very well." Here *swimming* is a participle. "His mother objects to his swimming alone." *Swimming* is a gerund in this sentence. (That's why HIS and not HIM swimming alone.)

Pseudo-Possessives.   They may not deserve it, but they get the customary apostrophe anyway: *A hard day's labor, hair's breath, two weeks' salary.*

Joint Possession.   If Jack and Jill jointly own a condo in Miami Beach, one apostrophe will do the trick: *Jack and Jill's condo*; if the ownership is separate, it's indicated by an apostrophe after each name: *Jack's and Jill's clothes.* About as logical as it gets.

Contractions.   We could hardly do without them, especially in informal writing; they add the flavor of living speech. Here the apostrophe, signifying obvious omissions, is the heavy hitter: *it's, isn't, haven't, weren't, wasn't, couldn't, shouldn't,* etc.

(George Bernard Shaw, one of the great prose writers of his time, had his own notion of punctuation. He disliked apostrophes in contractions and refused to use them, writing *dont, didnt, wont*. Being Shaw, he got away with it and his works are still printed that way.)

Omitted Letters.   Apostrophes mark omissions, as in *rock 'n' roll, you tell 'em, ne'er-do-well*.

Single Letter Plurals.   *Dot your i's, cross your t's. Learn the three R's. All B's on a report card. Oakland A's.* But not in multiple letter combinations: *His ABCs, VIPs.*

Buffer.   The apostrophe acts as a buffer between words ending in *s* or *s* sounds followed by a word that starts with *s. For goodness' sake, for conscience' sake.* (Otherwise: *For conscience's ease, for appearance's brevity.*)

Similarly: *The hostess' sense (the hostess's party); the witness' story (the witness's evasions).*

Double Possessive.   *Ken Lay was said to be a friend of Bush's.* Both the *of* and the *'s* at the end of Bush indicate possession, as they would in "an ally of Cheney's." The *'s*—the second possessive—isn't strictly necessary, but most authorities accept it and many writers use it: *a colleague of my father's, a customer of my mother's, a friend of mine, a buddy of my brother's.* Neither form is grammatically wrong.

Sometimes "of" standing alone can be ambiguous: *A portrait of Picasso*—a portrait of the painter or by him? Clearer is "a portrait of Picasso's."

Lifeless Ones.   Abstractions don't lend themselves easily to possessives (and don't sell well elsewhere). Therefore, *he is a benefactor of Harvard* (not *Harvard's* because, whatever Harvard may think, it's inanimate). *Smith is a big supporter of Clinton High School* (not *school's*, for the same reason).

Observe the obvious limitations, but remember we can—and do—use inanimate objects, especially when they are somewhat personified: *at death's door, the hurricane's power, the ocean's wildness.*

Indefinite Pronouns.   Possessives are formed conventionally: *somebody's grammar, anybody's game, everybody's favorite.*

Omitted Numbers,   as in the *Spirit of '76, Depression of the '30s, the giddy '20s.* But no apostrophe in such numbers as *F–16s, 757s.*

Description.   Don't use apostrophes in such primarily descriptive phrases as *a New York Mets outfielder, a teachers college, a writers manual, a childrens book, the agencies request.* As the AP Stylebook helpfully notes, the apostrophe is usually skipped if "for" or "by" would go better than "of" in a longer version: *college for teachers, manual for writers, request by the agencies.*

In descriptive names, some organizations or institutions use the apostrophe while others don't. Follow their practice. For instance, *Diners Club,* but *National Governors' Association.* Consult your house style.

Titles, Initials.   Conventional possessives, *'s. Henry VIII's hapless wives, Queen Elizabeth II's reign, William Simpson Jr.'s fourth bride.*

Dubious Deletions.   There are many, especially when writers try to reproduce dialect in print. A small instance will suffice: deletion of the terminal *g*, usually dropped from words in the South and other regions.

So quotes often appear: *"He said he liked fishin' and huntin', but today it was rainin'."*

The point is hard to see. I suggest you transcribe such words in standard English. As one Southern editor said, "Hell, if we did this all the time people drop the *g*, we'd run out of apostrophes."

Chapter 4
BRACKETS

They can't be transmitted by some computers, but most emphatically, they exist. Square where their cousins, parentheses, are round, you'll find them most often in print journalism. They are slightly more emphatic than parentheses.

Brackets are used around inserts of editorial matters in direct quotes—usually by way of explanation or clarification.

Brackets also work well in multi-point reports. To illustrate: Assume a report on the latest Mideast violence written by a reporter from Tel Aviv.

A bracketed paragraph inserts reaction and comment from Washington, D.C. Another provides material from Saudi Arabia. This information originated elsewhere and therefore could not have been included by the original reporters.

(In a pinch, you can substitute parentheses for brackets. And there are ways besides using brackets to handle out-of-origin information.)

Chapter 5
CAPITALIZATION

We now come to a subject that seems as large as the Grand Canyon and as spongy as Dismal Swamp.

Capitalization looms large when it includes, as it does in many style manuals, hundreds of words illustrating what's uppercase and what's lowercase. Offering that many particulars might make a little book by itself.

The subject is squishy because, unlike punctuation, it lacks logic. Capitalization is largely arbitrary, a matter of style and preferences, which vary among publications.

But then logic isn't the point of capitalization; the goal is consistency, and that's important enough.

Unlike the profuse offerings of some manuals, I lack the space to give you more than a terse view of general (not universal) practice. In any case, the question of upper and lowercase is not really a part of punctuation. It is a separate entity.

Relevant illustrations are legion, useful regularities scarce, and some of these are obvious. You need hardly be told that the first word of a sentence is capitalized, or that the days of the week are. You learned that in grade school.

And what compelling reason can anyone find for lowercasing, rather than capitalizing, "pope"? Or that "president" comes with a small *p*, while the capital letter held sway for so long and still does in some publications?

There are no conclusive answers to such questions. You can only shrug and follow one accepted version of capitalization, paying due attention to the prescriptions in a stylebook or dictionary.

I'll start my survey with the mother of all capitalization rules:

Proper Nouns.   Capitalize all nouns that name and identify all people, places and things: *Henry, Nigeria, New York, England, General Motors, Microsoft.*

Trademarks.   *Pepsi-Cola, Prestone.* You can't be expected to know them all, but when you lowercase a trademark you may get a letter from a lawyer gently asking you to reform.

Intellectual Property.   Titles of books, plays, movies, TV shows, artworks, songs, compositions are all capitalized (with quotation marks around them). *"A Farewell to Arms," "Larry King Live," Beethoven's "Eroica."*

Geographic Entities.   *Indonesia; Idaho; U.S. South; the Midwest; West Coast.* But: *The economy went south. He headed straight west. The city is south of Minneapolis.*

Government   takes itself seriously at all levels, as well it might; there seems to be a million components. Capitalize principal units: *White House, Congress, Senate, Capitol* (the building, not the city, *capital*). *Federal Aviation Agency, Supreme Court, Justice Department, State Department.*

On state and lower levels, capitalize the formal names of agencies, divisions and governmental units *(the Kansas Fish and Game*

Commission). Legislature is usually lowercase except formally as in *Missouri Legislature.*

Titles.   Before the full name, they are capitalized: *Secretary of State Colin Powell,* but *Colin Powell, secretary of state.*

Shirtsleeve Items.   By comparison with the starched form of titles, you have relaxed popular expressions, also capitalized: *Chicago's South Side, New York's Lower East Side, South Central district (Los Angeles), the Badlands, Philadelphia's Main Line.*

Religion.   Reverently capitalize all forms of divinity: *Allah, God, the Lord, Jehovah.*

Uppercase holy books, holy days, names of recognized faiths and denominations. *Judaism, Orthodox Jew, Reform Jew, Roman Catholic Church* (but not church itself), *Bible, Scriptures, Old Testament, Gospels, Quran.*

Also *Methodists, Episcopalians, Seventh-Day Adventists.*

Oddly, rituals are lowercased, as in *baptism, confession, sacrament, communion.*

Nautical. Capitalize the name of all ships: *Queen Elizabeth, U.S. Enterprise* (no quotation marks). *Navy,* as in *U.S. Navy,* but not "fleet."

Derivatives. *France* and *French* are upper-case, of course, but not *french fries* or *french toast, scotch and soda,* or *quixotic, pasteurize* or *venetian blinds.* These terms have drifted too far from the original meaning to require capitals.

Derivatives that depend on the proper noun for their meaning are capitalized: *Christianity, English, American, Marxism.*

Common Nouns. Humble nouns like river or street are promoted to uppercase when they are part of a full name: *Democratic Party, Missouri River, Wall Street.* Lowercase the second words when they stand alone—*the party, the river.* In Plurals, the common nouns stay common: *Republican and Democratic parties, Missouri and Kansas rivers, lakes Erie and Ontario.*

Historic Periods and Events are in suitable capitals: *Middle Ages, Renaissance, Industrial*

Revolution, Cultural Revolution, Prohibition, Civil War.

While on history, add historic or solemnly traditional speeches: *the Gettysburg Address, State of the Union Address, State of the State Address.*

From the playpen of sports: *the Kentucky Derby (the Derby* for short), *the World Series (the Series), Olympic Games, World Cup.*

Special Days.   *Presidents Day, Independence Day, Thanksgiving Day, Christmas, New Year's Eve, Mother's Day.*

So capitalize such occasions and celebrate.

Chapter 6
THE COLON

If the colon had a trademark, it might be (begging Dickens' pardon) "Great Expectations." Maybe the expectations might not be all that great—some would be picayune—but the colon is supposed to anticipate and then deliver the goods promised in the preceding sentence.

For instance:

The merger of Dementia Co. and Precox Inc., produced a surprise: The companies achieved those elusive synergies and the combined company registered higher profits than they showed individually.

The introductory sentence promises a surprise. The second, true to the colon, brings home the bacon.

This function affords some excitement, or as much as punctuation can achieve. Aside from having promises to keep, the colon has a lot of more mundane chores.

Summary.   One frequent use is the humble summary (or series).

The company's rosy profit picture emerged from: overly clever bookkeeping, flexible financial officers, gullible shareholders and perhaps downright fraud. Elements of the Republican platform: opposition to same-sex marriages and adoptions, sizable tax cuts and a stronger military.

(Note the capitalization of the first word after the colon ONLY if it is a proper noun or the start of a complete sentence.)

Handling Quotes.   When the quote is short, no more than one sentence, a comma is preferable: *The chief executive bellowed, "shareholders be damned."* Use the colon to introduce a quote that runs longer than a sentence, perhaps extends over several paragraphs.

No Colons.   Colons don't belong after a verb. *The companies in question are General Motors, General Electric and Ford. The philanthropist* *shelled out for many beneficiaries, including Johns Hopkins, the New York health service, Harvard and UCLA.*

(No colons.)

No colons, either, if a series follows such expressions as "for example," "namely," "that is," "such as." They effectively supplant the colon.

Listings.   Here the colon is endemic. Elapsed time: *1:32.7.* Time of day: *8:30 p.m.* In biblical citations, a colon separates the chapter and verse numbers: *Gen. 5:28.* Use colons also in subtitles of books: *"Voices: What Schizophrenics Hear and Why."*

Emphasis.   The colon seems an unlikely candidate for dramatic effect, but now and then it serves that purpose well: *Smith had only one passion: pornography of every sort.*

Dialogue Q. and A.   Colons are used in both.

Prosecutor: Is it true that you have a huge collection of pornography, child pornography included?

Defendant: *I'm proud of my collection, but children are never involved.*

Colons can also be helpful, though hardly mandatory, in the following specific cases:

Setting a Theme.   *His message was simple: Exterminate all juvenile delinquents.*

Explanation.   *Smith dropped his business at last: He had gone bankrupt three times, and the fourth time loomed.*

Conclusion.   *He gobbled down four sandwiches: He must have been hungry.*

Colons are also a neat bridge to explanations.

He'll have to wait seven months for full membership, though: The PGA Tour adopted a policy in September that players must be 18 before they can become members. Tryon turns 18 on June 2.

They are also useful in compressing complex proposals, policies and plans to their essentials.

The CEO's plan was this: Sell a million more cars per year, dismiss an unspecified number of workers by closing two divisions, try to whittle down suppliers' prices and sell several marginal businesses.

A more imaginative adaptation of the same idea was this lead-in to an article in The Economist:

Foreign policy: splendid but fragile. Economic reform: cautiously encouraging. Democracy: still wobbly. Stirrings of public spirit: small but detectable. That would crudely sum up the remarkable but contradictory changes in Russia, some of them apparent since Sept. 11.

I stand by my colons in this section and don't want to complicate things, but I should note that there are other possibilities. For example, the dash, though generally overused, can also introduce summaries. In some examples (not the last three), a period might work, too. You have to weigh the advantages before making your choice.

Chapter 7
THE COMMA

Commas aren't much to look at—not elegant like the exclamation point nor emphatic like the dash—but they handle enough major roles to qualify as virtuosos among punctuation marks.

And as temperamental performers, they need to be treated with respect and precision. They'll cause trouble when misplaced, as they often are, and cause even more trouble when they are erroneously omitted, from attribution, for instance:

In 1912 (,) he said (,) automobiles were fewer and slower. . .

He didn't say it in 1912. Without the commas, the sense evaporates.

Besides nurturing attributions, commas deftly separate clauses, clarify murky sentences, fence off appositives, asides and inessentials, organize series, sunder absolute verbs and direct addresses from the main sentence, and perform a fistful of other important chores.

Despite, or because of, the commas' versatility, they are easily overused. Here's an example from a book of quotations:

You can't derail a train by standing in front of it, or not quite. But a tiny bit of steel, properly placed . . .

All but one of those commas are unnecessary:

You can't derail a train by standing in front of it, or not quite. But a tiny bit of steel properly placed . . .

This first sentence was simple and short, though swollen with commas. Then there are writers addicted to piling on clauses by resorting to commas; writers who specialize in overlong, convoluted sentences of the sort that, in Alexander Pope's words, "like a wounded snake crawl along."

In Pope's days, incidentally, commas were in high fashion and appeared in gaudy profusion. Modern practice has marched in the opposite direction: The fewer commas, the better. Unneeded commas are anathema.

To encourage economizing, I have added a special section, "Doing Without," that summarizes where commas can and probably should be omitted.

Commas may not exactly be "our friends," as a recent style and grammar guide proclaims with a 21-gun salute, but you'll get along with them well enough, provided you understand their ways and avoid the traps they set for the inattentive.

And as the bereaved widow in "Death of a Salesman" says, "Attention must be paid." That applies to punctuation generally and doubly to the comma.

Compound Sentences.   When independent clauses are linked by conjunctions (but, and, yet, for, so, nor, neither) the conjunctions are always preceded by commas. This rule applies to compound sentences generally.

Terrorists might strike at any time, SO the government kept issuing warnings.

The company's sales kept dwindling, AND bankruptcy seemed ahead.

Either you pay, OR we'll have to cancel your seat.

Other compound-complex sentences:

The battle is on for those who see themselves as dispossessed, prey to joblessness and crime, AND open to the blandishments of the National Front.

Many millions have been spent on aid to Bangladesh, with its abject living standards, YET the effects of the nation's economy are invisible.

Since the latest operations began, the Israeli army has arrested more than 300 militants, AND about half were on Israel's wanted list, Defense Minister Ben-Eliezer said.

Dependent (Subordinate) Clauses   that march ahead of the main clause usually take a comma:

Written by the nation's top pornographer, the novel is sure to rack up big sales.

If it rains tomorrow as predicted, our backyard picnic will have to move indoors.

Also use a comma before a subordinate clause that brings up the rear of a sentence:

The president appeared in Keokuk this morning and discussed corporate scandals, SAYING THAT stronger enforcement was needed.

With Adjectives.   Commas are trundled out between adjectives that are NOT linked, for example in "a strong, aggressive military," or "a devious, fashionable banker." In neither set of adjectives is there a compelling relationship. Tip: If you can place an "and" between them (a "but" might be better in the second example), commas are superfluous.

Reverse Test.   You would not, while sane, insert "and" in the following expressions: "little old lady," "angry black dog" or "moth-eaten cloth coat," and so there's NO comma after the first adjective. They modify the subsequent noun phrases, such as "black dog" or "cloth coat."

Essentials/Nonessentials.   Grammar intrudes; sorry about that. Essential, or restricted, clauses and phrases make themselves indispensable. They are vital to the meaning and can't be dropped without spoiling it. Nonessential (nonrestrictive) elements add descriptive and secondary information and can be cut without damage. The significance, from our point of view: The essentials are never set off by commas, while the nonessentials require them. Examples:

Please hand me the book that's on the windowsill. (The "that" clause specifies the book and is restrictive; no commas.)

Please hand me that book, which has nice illustrations. (Nonrestrictive, mandatory comma before the "which.")

They visited the Victorian house where their grandparents had lived. (Essential, the clause defines the place.)

Democracy, despite its flaws, is the best government yet devised. (Nonrestrictive clause, with commas.)

One more point: In relative clauses, restrictives are introduced by "that," nonessentials by "which."

Appositives. When nonrestrictive, as they usually are, appositives are flanked by commas:

Lott, the Senate majority leader, is pouting in a corner.

Robert Satloff, executive director of the Institute for Near East Policy, said, "What is lacking from U.S. foreign policy is consequences for Arafat for refusing to fight terror."

No comma, of course, with a restrictive appositive:

The novelist Cynthia Ozick has written a great many books.

Missing Commas.   Forgetting a comma probably is more hazardous to your prose than misplacing it. In the following example, the writer forgot all about the second comma:

"It is clear we are working on a bankruptcy plan for Sabena," said Inge Verwotte, a union leader adding that management told them . . .

It wasn't any old union leader who added, it was Verwotte to whom the appositive applies. The proper comma after "leader" would make things clear. Another example:

It was amazing the percentage of people who are willing to give up freedom to get back some sense of security . . .

We are not amazing the percentage; a comma after the introductory "it was amazing" is essential.

Series.   Put commas to separate the elements of a series, but no comma goes before the final conjunction, as in "red, white and blue."

Nickodemus sold baseball stuf—bats, inscribed balls, hats, helmets and other memorabilia.

She couldn't decide whom to pick: The banker, the broker or the auto mechanic.

Introductory Clauses.   Unless they are very short, a few words, introductories are always followed by a comma:

When he tired of what was once called the "rat race" in New York, he packed up and moved to Vermont.

In this onetime coal town near the Belgian border, French pundits say an unlikely battle is developing.

Subject/Verb.   Never let a comma intervene between subject and verb: *Thomas Jefferson (,)* *died in the early 19th century. Pitcher Roger Clemens (,) has a mean fastball.* (The erroneous commas in both examples show a fairly common error.)

A CONTRACTOR operating a scaffold that collapsed at the John Hancock Center and killed three people when it crashed to the street below, VIOLATED manufacturer's specifications for using the equipment.

This sentence is awkward enough for the writer to forget that "violated" is the verb of the subject, "contractor." No comma after "below," therefore.

In Attribution. This is fairly routine and consistent. The only danger is in forgetting to put the commas where they belong.

A comma introduces a direct quote if it's a complete sentence within a paragraph. If it stretches longer, use a colon.

Two commas set off attribution in the middle of a sentence:

"We can't guarantee success," the spokesman said, "but we'll certainly try."

A comma goes at the end of a quote (unless there's a question mark or exclamation point there). *"We'll certainly try," the spokes-man said.*

Direct Address.   The requirement is simple enough, though often overlooked: Any form of direct address is always followed by a comma:

Beowulf, hand over that whiskey. Move over, Beethoven. Dad, you don't understand rock music.

Interjections.   However mild, asides and similar expressions that disturb the flow of thought all take commas:

Well, I predicted the recession. By all odds, you might have gone broke. Sorry, life is unfair. Why, where are you putting that comma? Regardless of your advice, I prefer not to go. By all that's sensible, don't wear that hat.

Sentence Adverbs.   Invariably followed by commas, sentence adverbs modify the entire following sentence. They also tend to be dull ("basically" and "essentially" especially), and, if you consider them carefully, useless.

Basically, my grandmother was a crook. Essentially, your grandiose plan is hogwash.

Frankly, the president's speech was a washout. Unfortunately, his checkered past can't be concealed from prospective employers.

Absolute Phrases. In case you wonder, these are participial phrases that may include a noun or pronoun, sport a subject or not. What they should always sport is a comma at the end.

Having been demoted from CEO, he gritted his teeth and left the company.

Her good looks having faded, so had her modeling career.

Speaking of mental health, where does our computer programmer stand?

The death penalty, generally speaking, is not always just.

Adverbial Clauses. At the start of a sentence, they are usually treated as garden-variety introductory clauses. In mid-sentence, they are set off by commas:

The burglar, after ransacking the apartment, made a smooth exit.

The military, in the chaotic nature of warfare, makes some regrettable mistakes.

Peripheral Matter. As already suggested in my discussion of nonrestrictive phrases, descriptive and peripheral material is set off by commas:

Osama bin Laden, it is believed, may or may not be dead. The mayor, who seems to be balding, has a haircut twice a week. The parents, while on a tight budget, sent their children to elite private schools.

Word Repetition. A comma separates identical words: *Whatever happens, happens. The problem is, is the funding adequate?*

Comma Magnets. Expressions like *of course, however, in fact, indeed, meanwhile* and their mates are usually set off by commas (not always; see "Doing Without" at the end of this chapter).

The defendant, of course, claimed he was innocent. They heard about the scientists and decided, therefore, to abandon their theory. The boy was lost a long time; however, he escaped without a scratch. The budget, in fact, was very tight. She rejected his overtures, and said, moreover, that she couldn't trust him. The official acknowledged that the situation was, indeed, a crisis.

Expressions like "for instance," "for example" and "namely" are set off by commas:

Henry Ford, for example, said that history was bunk. The security official said that New York, for instance, remained in the danger zone.

Hometowns and Ages. A person's hometown is set off by a comma when it appears in apposition to the name:

Harry Hasbeen, New Orleans, and Loretta Lacklustre, Chappaqua, N.Y. Age is also set off by commas: *Harry Hasbeen, 72, New Orleans.*

State, City Names. *Joe Journalist traveled from Fargo, N.D., to Birmingham, England. The Buffalo, N.Y., voters met with a representative in Washington.*

DOING WITHOUT

Here's a summary of examples when commas can be safely omitted and probably should be. But these are general suggestions, not "rules."

It's a good way, though, to avoid a comma excess.

Yet, Still.   Such adverbs are generally set off by commas, but they can be omitted in short sentences or clauses:

He was warned yet he persisted. Some Russians were opposed but nevertheless the stockpile was reduced. The economy was struggling and still there was no drop in employment.

Adverbial Phrases.   Initial adverbial phrases are generally, but not necessarily, set off by commas:

At dawn (,) they held an emergency meeting.
After breakfast (,) they departed.
In the end (,) they did what they had to do.
During training (,) his military ardor cooled.

Contraries.   Also known as antithetical statements, contraries need not always be set off by commas, especially when short:

The sooner the better. The more you whine the less you get. The greater the challenge the more the difficulty.

Perhaps?   Perhaps not. Words like "perhaps," "of course," "finally," "doubtless," "indeed" and other such quasi-commentaries are usually between commas. But not necessarily:

Perhaps the cardinal will resign. He was of course convicted of rape. It was doubtless an accident. The committee finally got down to business.

You can skip commas in longer sentences unless the expressions disrupt the thought or drift of the sentence:

We seem PERHAPS a tedious couple after all those swingers you've met.

They THEREFORE enjoyed the evening despite those charades and word games.

The company was IN FACT nearly broke when it announced a burst of solvency and profits.

Short Series.   When elements of a short series are linked by conjunctions but are short and simple, you don't need commas:

Maliciously she cited his failings: laziness and greed and arrogance. He considered himself a genius—brainy and creative and a compulsive worker.

Shared Subject. Never use a comma when two clauses share the same subject that's NOT repeated in the second clause:

They visited the museum and (they) ogled the dinosaurs.

You can skip the comma even if the subject is repeated:

THEY went to a diner where THEY feasted.

Adverbs. They don't necessarily require commas. Omit them when that makes sense to you.

Boldly (,) they decided to advance. Quietly (,) she got up and left. There (,) he was happy at last.

Reflexives. Commas in most cases are excessive:

They (,) themselves (,) participated. I (,) myself (,) am involved. Dr. Quack (,) himself (,) did the procedure.

If you keep the reflexives, consider recasting the sentence:

I am involved myself. They participated themselves.

No-Comma Zone.   No comma is used after an introductory adverbial phrase that's immediately followed by the verb it modifies:

IN AFRICA emerged the first faltering steps of human evolution.

OUT OF HER FANCY KITCHEN drifted some strangely repugnant odors.

Chapter 8

THE DASH

The time has come—alphabetically, anyway—
to consider the dash. It is a useful device, perhaps too useful; some commentators hold that
the dash is overused.

Be that as it may, the dash has a flair for
the dramatic—for example, by marking a decided change in the thought or direction of a
sentence. Otherwise, the dash performs more
humble, custodial chores.

Need a lead-in to a handy summary or list
within or at the end of a sentence? The dash is
at your service.

Need to insert secondary material? If it
deserves a little more emphasis than a mere
comma or parentheses, the dash will oblige.
Its main functions can be summarized
quickly.

Break in Thought. *On the worst possible day—what was I thinking of?—I hit the boss for a raise. Through her long reign, the queen and her family have adapted—usually skillfully—to the changing tastes of the time. He applied for and got the job—miraculously.*

Appositives. Use a pair of dashes when commas would be too feeble:

It was Attila—the most bloodthirsty among Hunnish leaders—whom they blamed for the destruction.

Summaries, Lists. Examples: *To meet her ultimatum, he packed frantically—two suits, shirts, socks, underwear, his favorite kitchen knife—while he worried about forgetting things. Teachers complained about missing essentials—desks, textbooks, pencils, chalk and even toilet paper. The official spoke of a leader who wouldn't lead, kept going back on his word, and rejected reasonable measures—he meant Arafat, though without naming him.*

Finale.   Use the dash before the final word of clause of a sentence to give it an extra lift:

She wanted to become a CEO—and she did. He wanted to avoid the authorities—and managed to slip past them.

Interruption.   A dash can signify an interrupted quotation:

Q. Would you explain your action?
A. Well, I didn't intend to—
Q. I asked about your action, not your intent.

Attribution.   Usually the memorable line of someone notable:

"A terrible beauty is born."
—William Butler Yeats.

Terminal Tips.   Introduce any series containing commas with a dash, not another comma. One more is too much.

One pair of dashes or a single dash in a sentence is enough. Don't overload with more.

Note. The dash doesn't hold a monopoly; at times, commas, colons, semicolons and even the lowly parentheses can fill its shoes. Sometimes dashes are clearly called for, sometimes it's a matter of nuance. It's a matter of informed choice.

Chapter 9
THE ELLIPSIS

An ellipsis is the conventional punctuation mark (. . .) indicating the omission of irrelevant parts of sentences, speeches, documents and other text. They can be useful when it comes to lengthy passages. Make sure, though, that what you leave out doesn't change the meaning of what's left standing.

Those three dots may be pretty, but ellipses should generally be avoided when possible—and it usually is. The direct, usually short quotes you see in news and feature articles hardly ever need ellipses. It's generally understood that quotes are excerpts from routinely drabber material. And you'll be well advised not to start or end a quote with an ellipsis.

When writers plunge into pointless ellipses, they sink far and fast. Here's a snippet from a news story:

"Why in God's name didn't . . . the top brass at Andersen immediately send out word to everyone . . . in the Enron case . . . not to touch a document, not to shred a document?" asked Rep. Jim Greenwood, the panel's chairman.

Greenwood seems to be stammering. What's missing is pretty clearly established by the context, and as so often a partial paraphrase will help you to avoid those ellipses and make for smoother reading:

Why didn't Andersen's top brass notify everyone in the Enron case "not to touch a document, not to shred a document?" asked Rep. Jim Greenwood, the panel's chairman.

Some ellipsis guidelines:

Highlights.   If the piece you're doing is largely a summary of highlights and capsulized key points, you won't need an ellipsis.

Typography.   If a grammatically complete sentence precedes an ellipsis, a period goes before the ellipsis. I doubt if any reader will count the dots or even pay attention to them, but if you go by the book, as you should, it will look like this:

"No, we haven't caught Osama bin Laden yet. . . ."

The period is in its accustomed place and the three dots come a space later.

Hesitation.   The ellipsis can express doubts and hesitations on a speaker's part:

"I'm not only ready to blame the umpire . . . I'm not sure what I'll do."

Trailing Off.   The ellipsis also serves to suggest a speaker's incompleteness of thought:

"I know that our divorce will serve our kids better, but . . ."

Adhesive.   You don't see it that often anymore, but the three dots have sometimes been used—in old-fashioned columns especially—to link disparate items.

In other events: A flower show at the Botanical Garden . . . A street fair in the West Village . . . A fashion show in midtown . . .

Chapter 10

THE EXCLAMATION POINT

Whatever qualities you impute to the exclamation point, subtlety isn't one of them. It works like a kettle drum, noisy but without nuances. Pain, fear, astonishment, anger, disgust—all in strong doses—are prerequisites for the exclamation sign.

"Ouch! My toes!" cries one, a bowling ball dropped on his foot. *"Somebody help me!"* screams a damsel in distress. *"Look, a real unicorn!"*

Astonishment.

"Get thee behind me, Satan!"

Rage and disgust.

You don't run into many emotional outbursts like these, so bang the drum slowly and very rarely. There are writers, misguided souls, who think than an exclamation point anywhere adds a dollop of emphasis.

But as a Time magazine style guide once said, "Punctuate the speaker's exclamations. Otherwise, write the emphasis into the sentence." Sound advice. But then what do you do with the exclamation points in this passage:

"Hezbollah accomplished these acts with impunity," Anderson said. "They got away with it! They weren't punished for it!"

You're witnessing the demolition of two perfectly good quotes—factual statements that needed nothing more than periods. They would have been even stronger that way.

Overfondness for the exclamation point results in the kind of breathless, excitable prose you can still find in some celebrity and gossip columns: *Richard is the sexiest man alive! She looked like a million dollars in her white gown!* and so forth ad nauseam.

A few further items will quickly fence the exclamation mark in.

Commands.   In addition to geniune exclamations, emphatic commands:

Put on your mukluks at once! Get away from that poisonous bottle!

Also interpolations, such as,

We rode through the Northwest—what a beautiful landscape!—in a Canadian train.

Irony. *The speaker contended that Hitler was a peaceful man. (!) Everyone knows how tolerant (!) the Taliban are.*

In Quotes. If the exclamation point is part of the quote, it goes inside the quotation mark and is never followed by a comma.

"I'm determined to be a suicide bomber!" she insisted.

Ambiguity. There's no intonation in print. So *"Oh, shut up"* may be uttered casually and pleasantly—or be a strong command. The exclamation point is usable only in the second case.

Reminder. This has been implied previously, but bears restating: Don't use an exclamation mark after MILD exclamatory sentences or MILD interjections. Use periods and commas instead.

Chapter 11
THE HYPHEN

Hyphens, Winston Churchill once wrote, are a "blemish to be avoided wherever possible."

Years later, the stylebook of the Oxford University Press put it more bluntly, observing that "if you take the hyphen seriously, you will surely go mad."

Such celebrated putdowns suggest that the hyphen deserves little respect, an attitude shared in modern practice: The fewer hyphens, the better.

After all, the hyphen is not a grammatical imperative. Within broad limits, its use is op-tional—left to the writer's taste, judgment and stylistic sense.

The hyphen's main job is to tell readers when combinations of two or more words should be understood as a single concept. The sole point is to insure clarity. When hyphens are not necessary for that purpose, consider them as Churchill did—a blemish.

Many compound modifiers need hyphens, especially in the scientific-technical field. Many don't.

You should clearly use hyphens in the following combinations, to avoid ambiguity:

Hard-working man, small-business operator, comic-strip artist, special-education teacher; patients-rights supervisor, nursing-home care, secret-weapons ban, 150-odd soldiers, special-interest money.

But only someone far gone with virulent hyphenitis would insist on hyphens in *high school teacher, income tax return, nuclear energy plant, intensive care unit, civil rights controversy, Social Security legislation, heart transplant surgeon.*

Nobody would misread modifiers like these and you don't need to clarify what's already clear.

Other Modifiers.   Hyphens are commonly used in compound adjectives such as *drought-stricken, rain-swollen, life-threatening, flood-ravaged, snow-covered, far-reaching.* The hyphens may not be strictly necessary to understanding, but they read better that way.

Guidance.   Any time you're in doubt about what and when to hyphenate, your friendly dictionary will be a dependable, though not infallible, guide.

Set Forms.   Word combinations that are usually hyphenated include *mother-in-law, half-baked, so-called, happy-go-lucky, pay-as-you-go, stick-in-the-mud, jack-in-the-box.* Here's a legitimate whopper: *weary, two-hands-aren't-enough mothers.*

Drop 'Em.   Hyphenated phrases that appear BEFORE a noun are unceremoniously stripped when the modifiers FOLLOW a noun:

First-quarter touchdown (touchdown in the first quarter); *she held a full-time job* (a job full time); *a well-qualified worker* (a worker well qualified).

Exceptions. There usually are, and this one is a little complicated: If a hyphenated modifier appears before a noun it RETAINS the hyphens afterward if it follows a form of the verb "to be."

An injury-prone player (a player who is injury-prone); *a much-traveled spy* (a spy who was much-traveled); *a fashion-obsessed tailor* (a tailor who is fashion-obsessed).

What's the deep grammatical rule for this? I can't say, but them's the rules.

Prefixes, Suffixes. Most of them are written solid. Hyphens are used to avoid doubling vowels or tripling consonants: *anti-inflation, bell-like, pre-entertainment*. It's *co-op* for clarity's sake, but no hyphens in *coordination* or *cooperation*, among others. *Quasi-, self-, all-* and *ex-* generally take hyphens: *quasi-scholar, all-encompassing, ex-plumber, self-conscious*.

Use hyphens to join a prefix to a capitalized word: *pro-British, un-American, pre-Columbian*.

Three suffixes come to mind: *-elect*, as in *president-elect; -like*, as in *Rehnquist-like*, and *-wise*, as in *media-wise* or *production-wise*.

I mention the third suffix with a shudder. It became popular over the past few decades, but -*wise* reeks of jargon and I urge you never to use it.

Paired Nationalities.   Hyphenated, as in these examples: *African-American, Italian-American, Chinese-Australian.* But *French Canadian* or *Latin American* go without hyphens.

Sweet Clarity.   That's why you hyphenate *co-op.* Also:

While the landlord was recovering, workers RE-COVERED the roof of his mansion. The sculptor was annoyed at having to RE-FORM the lump of clay.

With Single Letter.   Use a hyphen to link a capital letter to a word:

The executive sat behind his L-shaped desk. Sensitive people won't use the N-word.

Compound Verbs   are usually hyphenated: *cold-shoulder, blue-pencil, soft-pedal.* When unsure, look it up (in the dictionary).

With Numbers. *Twenty-four, 20–20 hindsight, 10–1 odds, 75-watt bulb, troops 10,000–15,000 strong.*

Hyphenate fractions when used as an adjective: *Two-thirds majority,* but not when used as a noun: *One fifth of his money disappeared.*

Suspended Hyphen. Retain the hyphen in constructions where only the final element is given:

They are the third- and the fourth-highest mountains in the range.

Strictly Verboten. Never follow an adverb ending in "ly" with a hyphen. It's *highly dangerous, intelligently conducted, beautifully done.*

If you have plodded through this welter of pointers and suggestions and turn to the larger world of print, you'll notice a curious phenomenon. A number of writers and editors will cheerfully ignore some of our precepts. But that's hyphenation: Consistency is not a major part of it.

Still, it is useful to know the general practice and customs, and sticking with them is probably the safest course.

As to the lack of unbending rules of correctness, the absence of a fixed star to steer by in all contingencies, let me add a final quote.

The formidable H. G. Fowler starts his discussion of hyphenation in his usage dictionary with an uncharacteristic disclaimer. He won't attempt, he says, to describe the hyphen's modern usage because "its infinite variety defies description. No two dictionaries and no two sets of style rules would be found to give consistently the same advice."

If even the omniscient Fowler couldn't bring the hyphen to heel, what mortal can?

Chapter 12
PARENTHESES

Parentheses preside over the peripheral—information not always trivial but never vital: asides and afterthoughts, comments, bits of background. Drop these snippets into the relevant sentence, without, however, disturbing its grammar and syntax.

Parentheses are useful for many purposes, among them to clarify an ambiguous pronoun and to translate technical and obscure terms into everyday English. But they are distracting, and should be avoided when possible. Commas and dashes can also do the job of parentheses, often more effectively.

The following examples show parentheses at work:

Mozart's last three operas (written in the summer of 1778) are considered among his strongest.

Fiction led the best seller list (with self-help books second).

He was so proud of his car (a 1998 convertible) that he let no one else drive it.

T. S. Eliot's "The Wasteland" introduced startling technical innovations to literature (like "Ulysses").

He was first arrested (he never forgot the date) on July 2, his 24th birthday.

Note the punctuation. All but one of the parenthetical sentences are incomplete, so no uppercase at the start and no period at the end. Even a complete sentence (last example) gets the same treatment if its meaning depends on the surrounding material.

A quick survey of how parentheses are used:

Translation.   *The applicant failed, because he was diagnosed as dyslexic and dysgraphic (unable to read and write). The patient was thought to have had a coronary thrombosis (heart attack). The unread poet blamed his troubles on the zeitgeist (spirit of the times).*

Who's He?   *The Republicans claimed (Senate Majority Leader) Trent Lott had undermined. . . . Among the speakers was (former New York Gov.) Mario Cuomo.*

Irritant.   Parentheses can be a major annoyance when they are dragged in to explain or clarify what needs neither.

She said she had written to the IRS, her senators, several agencies and even to (President) Clinton.

Could any reader on this planet NOT know that Clinton was president, especially in the context?

Road rage has become widespread, he said, and it wasn't uncommon that a furious driver pulled a gun on another. They (motorists) need to calm down . . .

Could he have been talking about sky divers?

Pronoun Aid.   *"There's no question that he has done a lot of work,"* the quote says. If a preceding passage mentions several people who might fit the pronoun, name the antecedent: *"that he (Smith) has done a lot of work."*

Nicknames.   *Shaquille (Shaq) O'Neal; Michael (Moose) Mussina.*

Location.   *He worked for the Baltimore (Md.) Sun. They visited the Baltimore, Md., aquarium. Use the first form for proper nouns only.*

Amplification.   *She rode a camel through the streets of St. Petersburg (known as Leningrad in the Soviet era).*

Conversion.   *"The sound was so loud I think you could have heard it from 10 kilometers (six miles) away," the policeman said.*

Chapter 13
THE PERIOD

The period is a mere dot in the panorama of punctuation, but it packs an impressive punch. Unlike, say, the colon or semicolon, it can bring a sentence to a complete halt.

That's why the British call the period a "full stop," and why an editor once called it "a great aid to sanity." To make his point, he sent a staffer who was overly fond of clauses a page-full of period dots. The writer's sentences became less elephantine.

Another prose savant, William Zinsser, commented that "not much is to be said about the period except that some writers don't come to it too soon."

Touché. In some sense, the period is a disciplinarian of style; it's a guillotine for the kind of sentence that, in Alexander Pope's words, crawls "like a wounded snake drags its slow length along."

Almost everybody concedes that a steady admixture of short sentences makes for readable prose. So keep those periods handy.

After that truism, let's advance to a quick summation:

Finality.   The period marks the end of a sentence and, for that matter, a sentence fragment:

Osama bin Laden has given a good imitation of the devil. To the West, at least. The war on terrorism is serious business.

Mild imperative sentences, rhetorical and indirect questions, all end in a period.

Don't forget to close the door. Why don't we just have lunch. She asked whether Colorado Springs was still in Colorado.

Initials.   No periods between well-known initials, such as *LBJ, JFK, FDR, CIA, FBI, UN, FCC, FAA.*

Abbreviations.   There are too many to list here. The most common ones: *Gov., Lt. Gov.,*

Sen., Mr., Mrs., Ms. For military service, corporate and other abbreviations, consult your style guide.

Numerals. In enumerations, *1. 2. 3.* Or with letters, *A. B. C.*

With that, we can put a period to the period.

Chapter 14
THE QUESTION MARK

The question mark is the least demanding of punctuation signs. All you need to know is what a question is and you punctuate accordingly.

How old are you?
Are you still running the sweatshop?
Will the terrorists strike again?

Not much doubt about those. They are direct questions, invariably followed by the interrogation point. But things aren't always that simple, as my case-by-case summary will show.

Indirect Questions. Never use a question mark after indirect questions:

The waiter asked whether he wanted baked snails or crispy frogs' legs. She wondered whether anyone could find the truth. He asked if she wanted more chocolate cake.

Question or Not? Consider this sentence: *You don't really want to go out in a storm like this.*

This could be merely a casual expression of mild disapproval, in which case the period is appropriate. But it could also be an urgent direct question. Only the question mark could tell.

In short, don't raise a question when no answer is expected.

"Would you mind closing the window" is framed like a question but probably isn't. The same applies to, *"Would you please not bang the door when you leave."* But:

"Would you please cut my horrid toenails?" requires an answer (probably negative).

Multiple Questions. You have two ways to handle them.

What were her vacation plans? Beach? Tennis? Reading "War and Peace"? Travel?

The other way would be to put one question mark at the end:

. . . Beach, tennis, reading "War and Peace," travel?

Endgame.   Attributive phrases are usually set off by commas, but NOT after a question mark:

"Who could have done such a thing?" she asked.

It's the same in the middle of a sentence:

Thoroughly puzzled, "Who could have done such a thing?" she wondered, staring at the wall.

Within a Question.   Questions inside an interrogative sentence need to be followed immediately by a question mark:

Did Le Pen really say that the Holocaust was a detail of history? Chirac was asked.

Interpolation.   *Suddenly my grouch of a boss—can anyone figure?—gave me a decent raise.*

Doubt.   A question mark within parentheses is also used to indicate uncertainty and doubt.

She said the accident may have occurred in 1989 (?).

Chapter 15
QUOTATION MARKS

Quotation marks are surely the most bland and colorless of punctuation signs. They hardly ever cause disputes, even among grammarians. Language commentators pick other targets. Linguists and lexicographers leave them in peace.

No mystery attaches to quotation marks, as it does now and then to the comma. For color or drama, you need to go to the dash and exclamation point.

Everybody who writes or reads knows where quotation marks go: around any form of direct speech and excerpts from texts. (If you run a full text, no quote marks are needed.)

By themselves, quote marks present no problem. What's between them is another matter. It's betraying no trade secret to note that too often quotes are pedestrian, wordy and predictable. But that's a question of editorial judgment, not punctuation.

Quote what's unusual, striking or original, not what's ordinary and routine. When then-Gov. Ann Richards said that George Bush was "born with a silver shoe" in his mouth, reporters had an emerald; had she said "silver spoon," they'd have had a glass bead.

Such quotes are rare to come by, but that's no reason for overquoting the unexceptional. An example:

Pentagon spokeswoman Virginia Clark said that "hard-core" al-Qaeda fighters were putting up "tough resistance" in the eastern Tora Bora region Monday. Fighting in the area was "intense," she said, and there was no indication "this was near the end."

None of these words and phrases needs to be quoted.

When quotation marks signal a human voice, readers expect something more vivid than a dry, factual recital:

"I was born in Minneapolis in 1935, attended the University of Iowa and moved to New York. . . . "

In quotes? No, thanks.

Another verboten: If you decide to use a cliche—"no one will touch that issue with a 10-foot pole"—never enshrine the cliche in quotation marks. That merely calls attention to it, and it's silly to imply a superior air to something you have just written.

More important: Quotes should advance your narrative, not merely embellish it, and arrange your quotes so that readers will always know who is speaking.

Don't fall for the myth that anything becomes automatically interesting if it's between quote marks. It never works that way, unfortunately.

A summary showing how quotation marks work:

Hands Off. If a statement is enclosed in quotation marks, it must be exactly what the speaker said. You can't "improve" it by changing words or phrases. Grammatical and other errors are the speaker's problems, not yours.

First Aid. Well, not just the speaker's problem. But nobody says you have to use a poor, confusing quote. You have two choices: 1. You paraphrase the statement in your own words, without changing the meaning; or 2. You drop the quote entirely.

Direct Speech.   That's the chief employer of quotation marks:

"I think that Enron's top management blew it," he said.

"It's terrible that many civilians were killed in the air attack," the spokesman said, "but some of this seems unavoidable."

The lawyer said that his client was "neither a model citizen nor a villain."

Note the standard punctuation. No quote marks in indirect speech: *The lawyer insisted that his client was neither a model citizen nor a villain.*

Fragments.   Mini-quotations, of one to about three words, tend to be fatuous and therefore undesirable:

The reviewer called the novel "well-done." Some members of the audience said they "greatly disliked" the play.

Justified Fragments. The tiny quotes are justified when writers need to dissociate themselves from controversial language or when the precise wording is significant in a legal, diplomatic or military context. For example:

The president said it was "absolutely necessary" to get rid of Saddam Hussein. (The exact phrase is important.)

Paris police identified the man as a member of "neo-Nazi and hooligan groups." (The police say that and may even know; the writer can't.)

Phantom Words. However plausible they may seem, don't ascribe words to speakers that they didn't exactly say. For instance, *Sen. Vladimir Blowhard says, "Most of us politicians have a serious problem with that issue."* The quotation has him say, "WE have a serious problem with that issue." The fact is that the speaker never said "we." Rephrasing is easy: *Blowhard said that politicians like himself "had a serious problem with that issue."*

Quotes Within Quotes. The mark is ('):
"I've always thought T. S. Eliot's 'Wasteland'

portrayed our declining society, but 'piffle' is what Eliot might have said to my analysis."

Broken-Back Quotes. *"Sometime soon, the political maneuvering," the senator said, "will have to come to an end." "This warrant," the lawyer said, "is completely without merit."*

Let the speakers complete their thought and keep the sentence flowing. Don't drop attribution into the middle of a statement unless it's a place where the speaker would naturally pause. In general, attribution should go at the beginning or the end of a quote.

Irony. Hard to define, but easy to spot. *Police found that the "big fight" was a brief barroom scuffle.*

OK, "big fight" is (primitive) irony, properly indicated by the quote marks. The danger is in marking off words when no irony is intended:

The general said all those American volunteers were "true patriots."

He meant it.

Inside, Outside?   Commas and periods always go inside quotation marks, although they can be replaced on that spot by an exclamation point or question mark. Normally, these two, as well as the dash and the semicolon, go outside the quotation, unless they are part of the quoted statement.

Didn't Shakespeare have Mark Anthony say, "I have come to bury Caesar, not to praise him"?

(Outside, because the question mark applies to the whole sentence.)

Gertrude Stein once asked, "What is the question?"

(Inside; part of the quote.)

Dialogue.   Always in quotation marks:

"Should you wear red socks?"

"They go well with my purple pants."

No quotation marks, however, in a formal Q. and A.

Titles.   Much more majestic than nicknames are the titles of various intellectual properties. Quotation marks, please, around the following titles: books, articles, operas, musical compositions, paintings, sculptures, plays, movies, songs, television shows.

"A Farewell to Arms," "Aida," "Death of a Salesman," Beethoven's "Eroica Symphony," Michelangelo's "David," Van Gogh's "Starry Night," "Nightline," "The Simpsons."

In compositions, when the number is not part of the formal title, no quotation marks: *Beethoven's Seventh Symphony, Rachmaninoff's Third Piano Concerto.*

So-Called   is usually the equivalent of quotation marks. Use one or the other, but not both.

Chapter 16
THE SEMICOLON

The semicolon is a compromise. It drifts, somewhat nebulously, between the period and the comma. To be pedantic, the semicolon means a shorter pause than the period and a longer pause than the comma.

Long or short pause, good stylists try to avoid it as too formal; decked out, as it were, in a starched shirt and a black suit. You would do well to keep semicolons at a minimum. There usually are options.

But wraith-like as it seems, the semicolon has dug itself a firm niche in punctuation. It serves to link independent clauses sharing the same general ideas. It can subdue a blizzard of commas. And it needs to appear before certain transitional words.

"*My husband has turned out to be such an ill-tempered crank that I am considering divorce; it's my only course, really.*"

Schmidt was cautious and accurate in the use of his sources; he was free of chauvinism.

"*Get back to bed and rest; I'll take the kids to school.*"

Periods or commas would not work as well as the semicolon here.

Obligatory. Do not use semicolons before coordinating conjunctions such as "and," "for" or "but"—UNLESS there is extensive punctuation in one or more of the individual clauses.

Mitzi obsessed about the dazzling Rodolfo; however, he seldom gave her any thought at all.

The plant was ill-lit, with barred windows, a creaky floor and a staircase that led to a front door, usually locked; moreover, the workers were paid a substandard pittance.

The semicolon needs to precede "moreover," but here it also spells relief from an overload of commas.

Tightwad is survived by his wife, Eulalia, a sister, Abigail Wilkinse of Fairbanks, Neb., a brother, Bruno, of Portland, Ore., and a nephew, Percy Hardscrabble, also of Portland; and three sons by a woman not exactly his wife.

The semicolon before the conjunction helps clear up the series and spares readers an additional comma.

No semicolon in the following, because of the coordinating conjunction:

The police officer didn't like the man's looks, but didn't do anything about it.

Synergy is a constant corporate hope—perhaps a myth, for it has seldom been realized after a large merger.

Chapter 17
THE SLASH

A single diagonal, the slash is not used correctly by all computers. Mechanically, it is used to denote the ends of a line in quoted poetry, or shows up in fractions, 2/3 etc.

More important, the slash is a punctuation mark that sprouts in legal and commercial jargon ("and/or") and should not be used outside these linguistic ghettos.

The troops proved to be ill-trained and/or ineffective.

The "or" by itself would lead many readers to assume that troops were both. But if you want to make it absolutely sure, *"ill-trained AND ineffective"* would do it.

A hint of legitimacy for the slash seems to appear in *"a sentence of one year's imprisonment and/or a $300 fine."* Here, just make it,

". . . of one year's imprisonment, a $300 fine or both."

Theodore Bernstein, in "The Careful Writer," calls the "and/or" formula "a visual and mental monstrosity that should be avoided."

That about sums it up.